Meet The Family

To make this guide as fun and colourful as can
be, assign everyone in your travel party a
...
...vourite
...d more
...colours

Savings

It's time to start saving for your dream vacation! Enter your target amount at the top of the thermometer and fill in some checkpoints on the right. Then you can colour in the thermometer as you get closer and closer to your target.

If budget is a big factor in your vacation planning, turn to page 51 in *Dream Guide* for help in deciding how to choose the cheapest time of year or page 77 if you'd like to learn how to book your dream vacation yourself and potentially save some money.

I personally tend to book my vacation and pay it off in increments. For example, I'll book my resort hotel, then pay $200 to Disney every month or so. You can choose to use this page to keep track of how much you've paid.

FUN FACT

In the 1940s scene of Walt Disney's Carousel of Progress, Jimmy is carving a pumpkin from a photo of his sister. If you look closely, you'll see that the photo, is just a picture of the Patricia animatronic, in the same exact scene! She's even holding the phone.

Our Vacation

DATE OF *Departure*

DATE OF *Return*

FUN FACT

At the end of Jungle Cruise, you'll meet Trader Sam. Take a look at his trousers and how they're a bright red and white. Well, they're made from the material that used to top the boats of the Jungle Cruise! Skippers realised that a boat would be easily spotted with a red and white roof, so when imagineers fitted the boats with the now khaki like material, they kept some of the old material for Sam.

Home Away From Home

Where is your home away from home going to be? Think of all the cozy nights you'll be spending in a freshly made bed, just moments away from the magic of Disney!

Here's some space for you to jot down your reservation details, as well as the contact information for your travel or booking agent.

RESORT HOTEL:

RES NUMBER:

AGENT NAME:

PHONE:

Flights

Outbound

From	Terminal	To	Terminal

Flight No.	Departure Time	Arrival Time	Baggage Allowance

Return

From	Terminal	To	Terminal

Flight No.	Departure Time	Arrival Time	Baggage Allowance

PRO TIP

When booking fast passes, start at the end of your vacation and work your way back. Fewer people have access to those end days, meaning you'll have less competition to get the best attractions and times.

Before we start getting down to business, let your imagination run wild! Fill up these wish lists with all the things you would love to do on your dream vacation. Then, you can go back through your wish lists and rank everything as a numbered priority.

This is also a good time to put your colour assignments to use. A great way to make sure everyone has a magical time, is to allow everyone a 'Must Do.' You can decide the rules yourselves but I'd recommend giving everyone at least one opportunity to say 'this is my favourite and we have to do this for me.'

Below is an example of how you can fill out the wish lists and overleaf you'll find a little explanation behind each header icon.

Name of Item　　　**Priority Rank**　　　**Favourite of...**

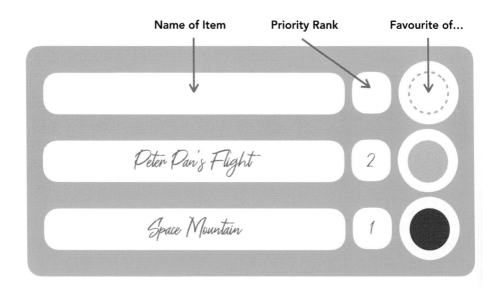

Peter Pan's Flight	2	
Space Mountain	1	

DINING OPTIONS

We all love Disney food! Now you can make a wish list of all the possible restaurants and quick service locations you might like to dine at over the course of your vacation.

SHOWS

From Voices of Liberty through to Disney Festival of Fantasy Parade, there are so many amazing shows to choose from.

ATTRACTIONS

This wish list might be the trickiest to write... since there's just so many amazing attractions to choose from! I'd recommend letting everyone choose at least one or two to start off with.

CHARACTERS

Characters are a big part of the Disney experience. Maybe you'll want to meet your favourite character or perhaps one you've never met before? Compile a wish list of your family's ideal meet & greets.

NIGHTTIME SPECTACULARS

Whether it's Happily Ever After or the Tree of Life nighttime Awakening, you've got some fantastic evening shows to end your days in the parks. Add in the one's you'd most like to see.

ADDITIONAL

Everyone's got something obscure they love about Walt Disney World. On this wish list, you can add the things you'd love to do outside of the normal parameters (e.g. 'walk around Grand Floridian').

FUN FACT

Early designs for Epcot actually included a Mount Fuji roller coaster in the Japan pavilion. However, Disney had a long standing relationship with Kodak Cameras at the time and Kodak weren't too happy with the idea of Disney indirectly advertising their competitor, Fujifilm.

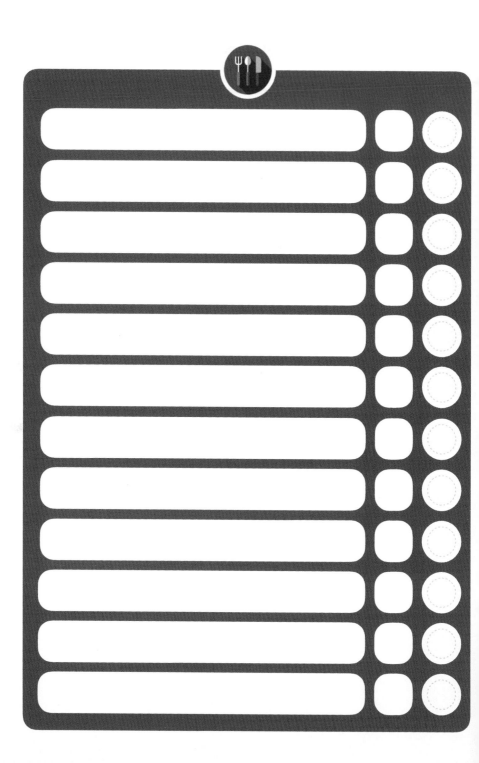

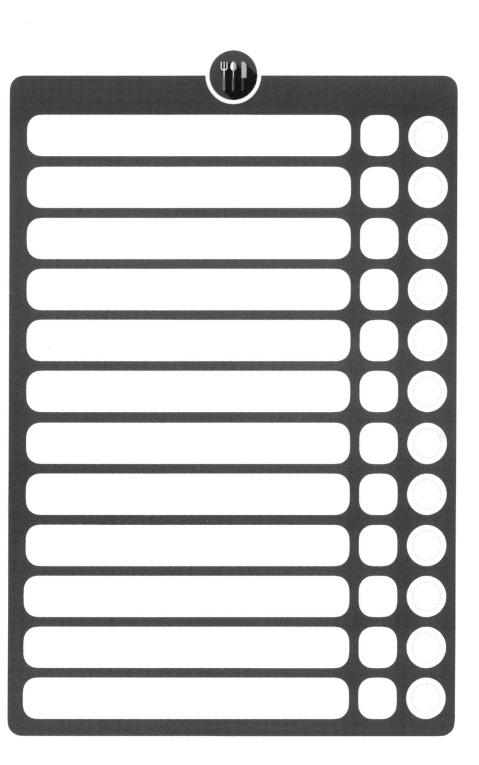

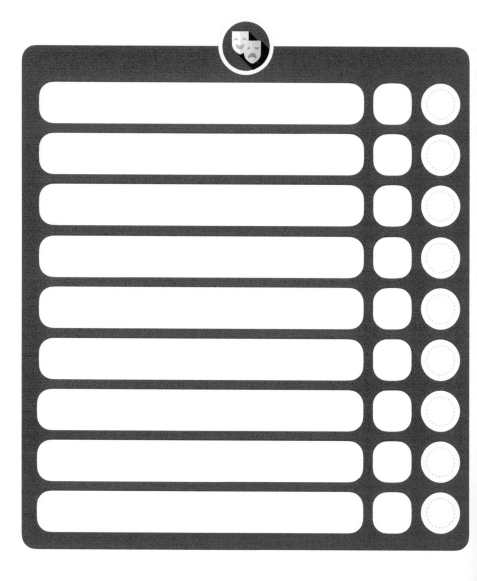

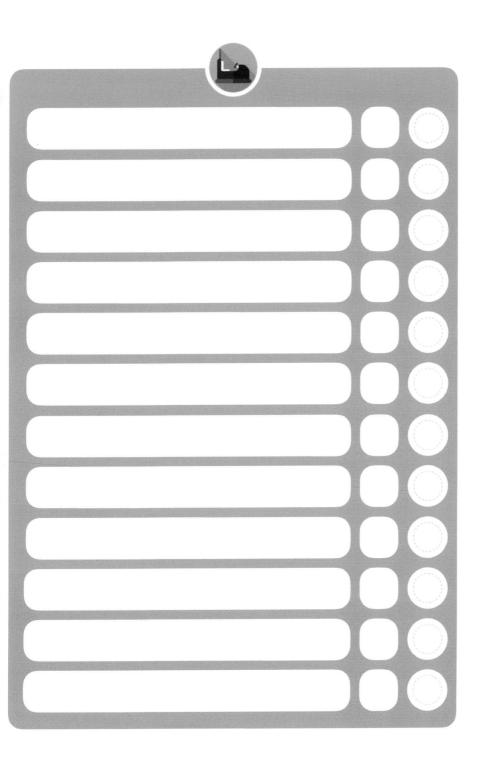

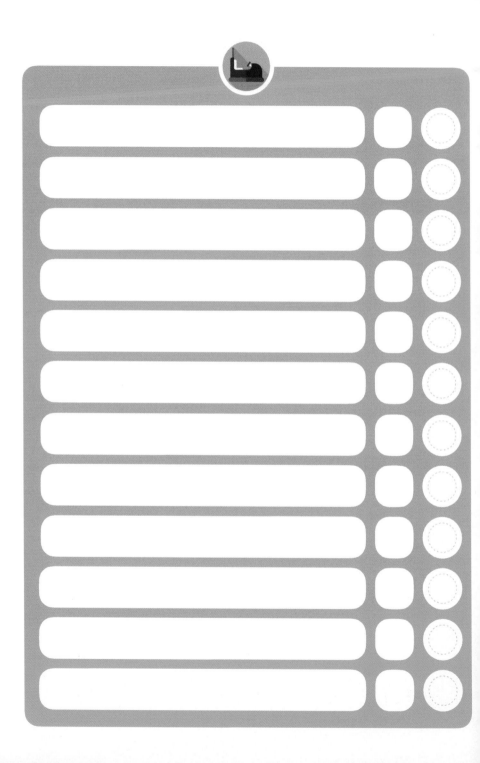

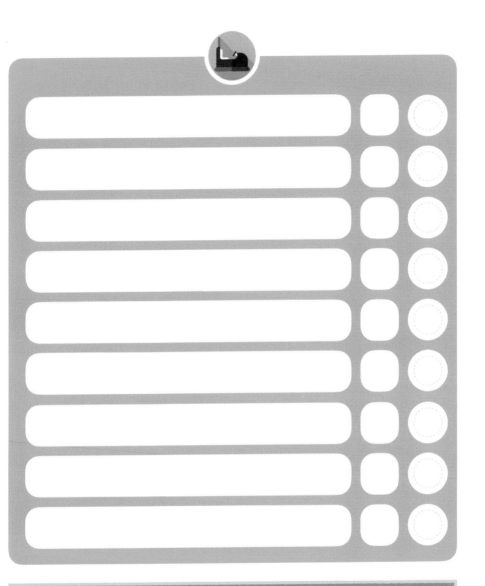

FUN FACT

You can actually live on Walt Disney World property (if you have the money). Golden Oak, is a luxury housing complex located between Fort Wilderness and Port Orleans Riverside. A house here might set you back a few million but they really are something special!

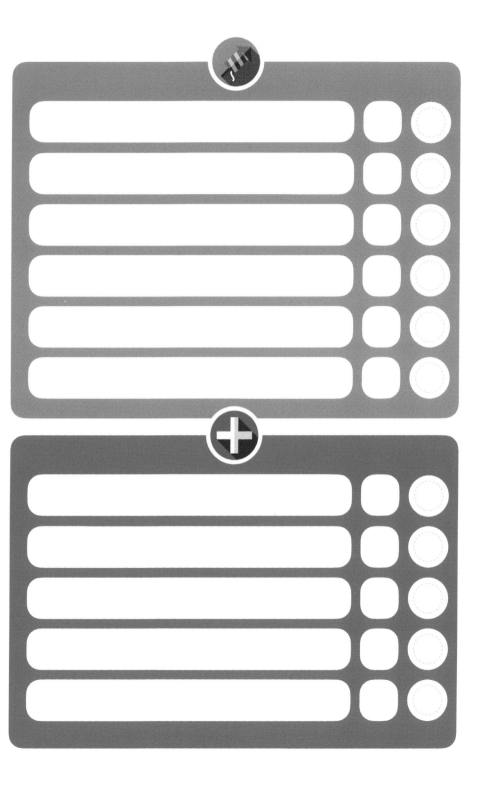

Day Planners

Now let's get down to the nitty gritty! You've written your wish lists, now's the time to go back through them and prioritise each item. With that, you'll be better prepared for organising your days and making reservations.

Whilst you're writing your day planners, it's a good idea to have My Disney Experience (MDE) open. Visit page 69 in *Dream Guide* for all the best advice on using MDE or for more information about what exactly it is.

The day planners are where you'll be able to turn those wish list items into actual fast pass and dining reservations. I'd also recommend having the Walt Disney World website open to check show times and opening hours during your vacation.

HOW TO DAY PLAN

I believe the planning process should be as fun and simple as possible. Sure, you could plan every hour of every day but that doesn't sound like much of a vacation to me and hasn't worked out when I've tried it in the past.

What I've done is give you some basic spaces to plan out the main elements of your days in Disney. Overleaf, you'll see what each of these spaces are for and I've provided some instructions on how to fill out each section per day. Not only that, I've also filled in one day as an example for you.

Don't stress too much about filling everything in at once. The planning of an entire vacation can't be done in a day. Especially when you'll have to book your dining reservations months before your fast passes. My advice, use a pencil when you start.

DATE & DAY

It's very easy on vacation to forget which day it is. I've provided space for you to also note which day of your vacation you're planning (e.g. Day 4).

DESTINATIONS

Here you'll find space to allocate up to two parks or destinations you're planning on visiting that day and their opening times.

FAST PASSES

Once you've booked your fast passes, note the three attraction names and your return windows in this space.

DINING PLANS

Here you can note down what you're doing for your meals. If you have a reservation, you can write the time in the space provided on the right.

SHOWS

Note down which shows you'd like to see. I wouldn't worry about times, since there's normally multiple performances per day and times vary a lot.

NIGHTTIME SPECTACULAR

No doubt you'll be wanting to see something special before you head to bed. Write the name of the spectacular you'll be seeing that night.

ADDITIONAL

Maybe you're planning to have some pool time, or maybe you want to pop to Disney Springs at night? Here's a space for anything you like.

PRO TIP

If you're struggling to get the dining reservations you want, fear not! A lot of guests cancel their dining reservations the day before. If you can't book what you want right now, be sure to check on My Disney Experience during your vacation for some great dining options.

DAY   Monday

DAY   4

DATE   14th April 2019

Disney Springs   10:00am to 12:00am

Epcot   9:00am to 9:00pm

FP

1 Frozen Ever After

3:05pm to 4:05pm

2 Spaceship Earth

4:15pm to 5:15pm

3 Living with the Land

6:00pm to 7:00pm

Breakfast

Gasparilla Grill

Lunch

Earl of Sandwich

Dinner   7:15pm

Rose & Crown: Dining Room

1   Pixar Film Festival

2   British Revolution

Epcot Forever   @   9:00pm

Visit the Days of Christmas Store.

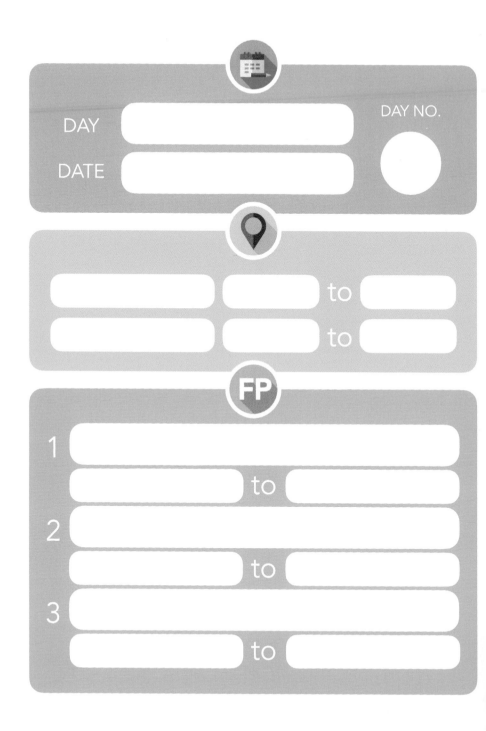

DAY

DATE

DAY NO.

to

to

FP

1

to

2

to

3

to

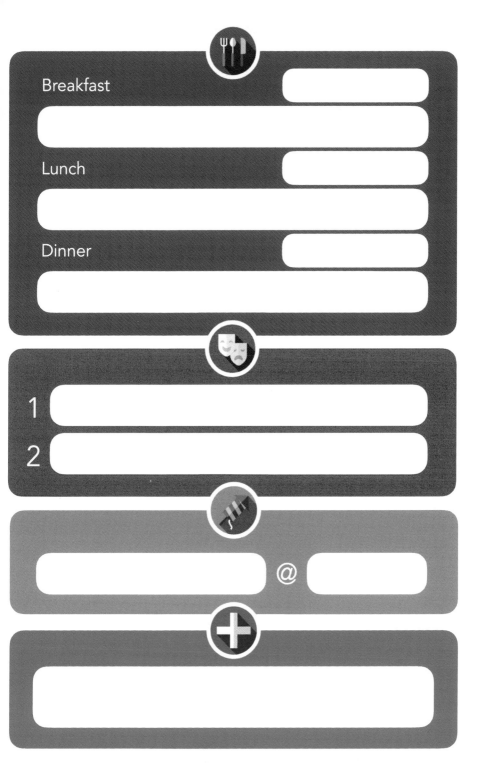

Breakfast

Lunch

Dinner

1

2

@

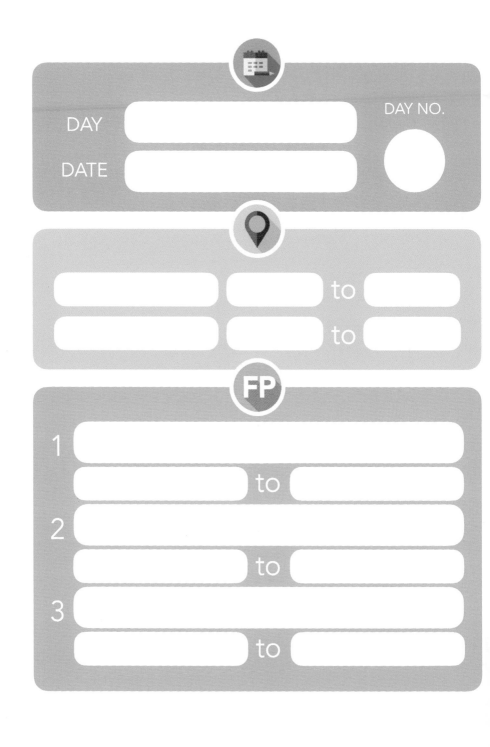

DAY

DATE

DAY NO.

to

to

FP

1

to

2

to

3

to

Breakfast

Lunch

Dinner

1

2

@

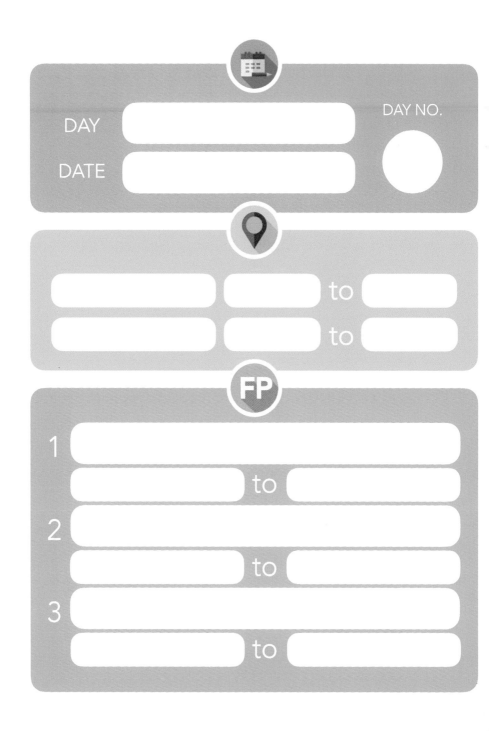

DAY

DATE

DAY NO.

to

to

FP

1

to

2

to

3

to

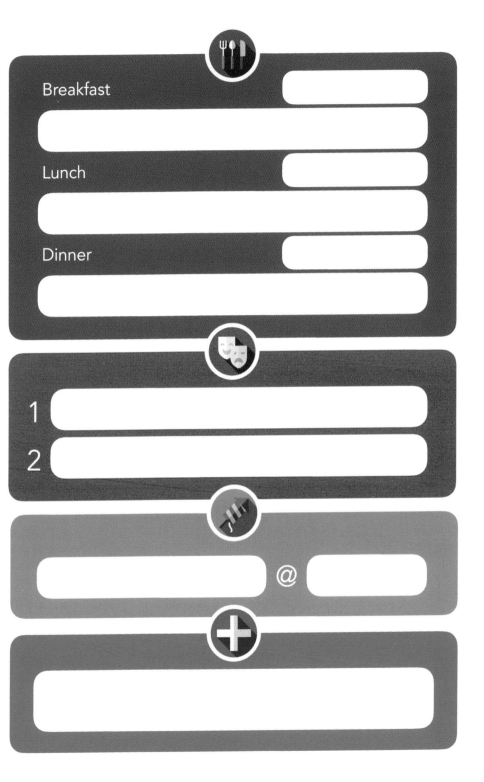

Breakfast

Lunch

Dinner

1

2

@

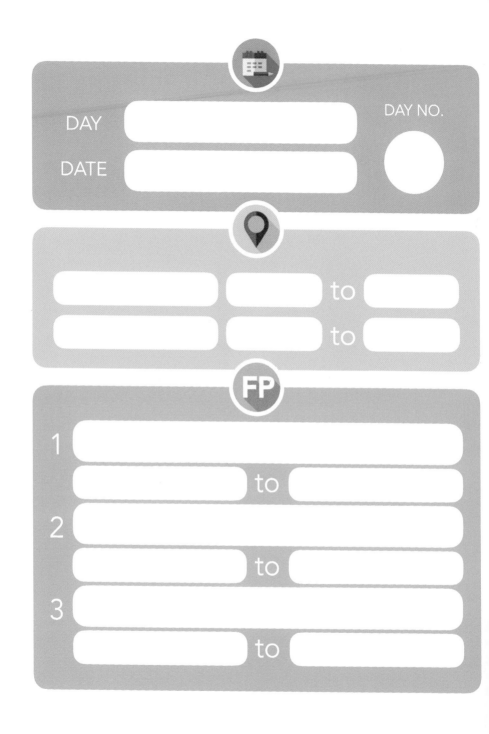

DAY

DATE

DAY NO.

to

to

FP

1

to

2

to

3

to

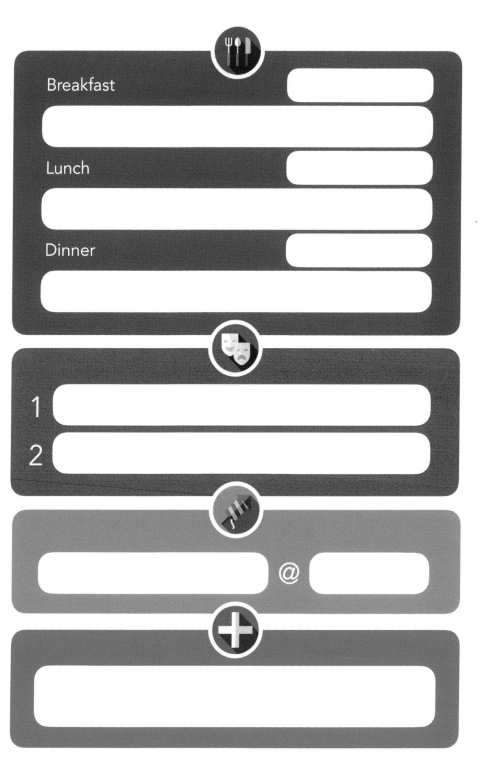

Breakfast

Lunch

Dinner

1

2

@

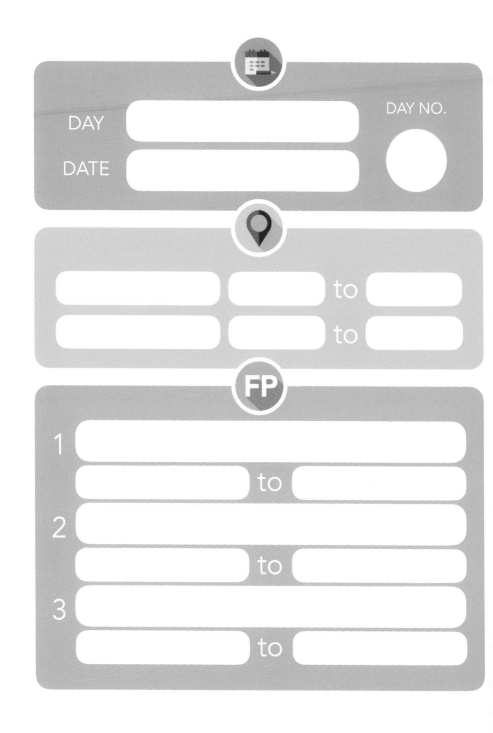

DAY

DATE

DAY NO.

to

to

FP

1

to

2

to

3

to

Breakfast

Lunch

Dinner

1

2

@

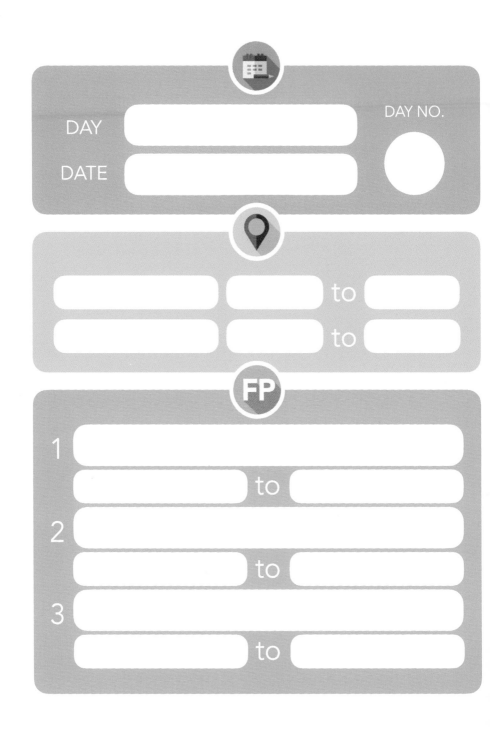

DAY

DATE

DAY NO.

FP

1 _____ to _____

2 _____ to _____

3 _____ to _____

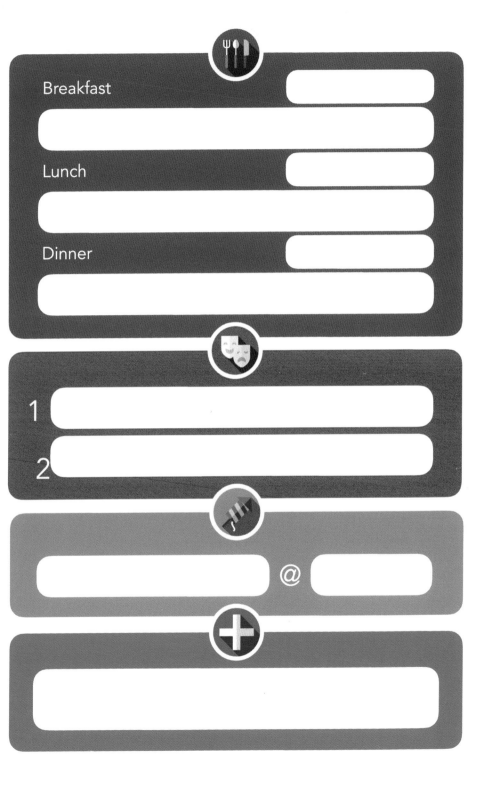

Breakfast

Lunch

Dinner

1

2

@

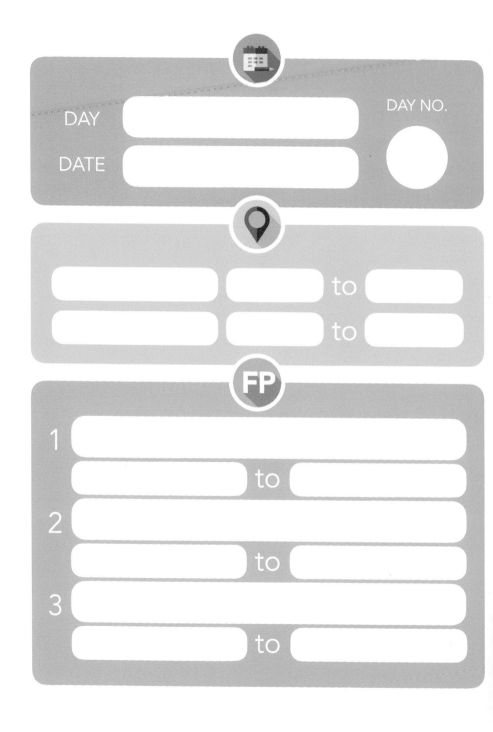

DAY

DATE

DAY NO.

to

to

FP

1

to

2

to

3

to

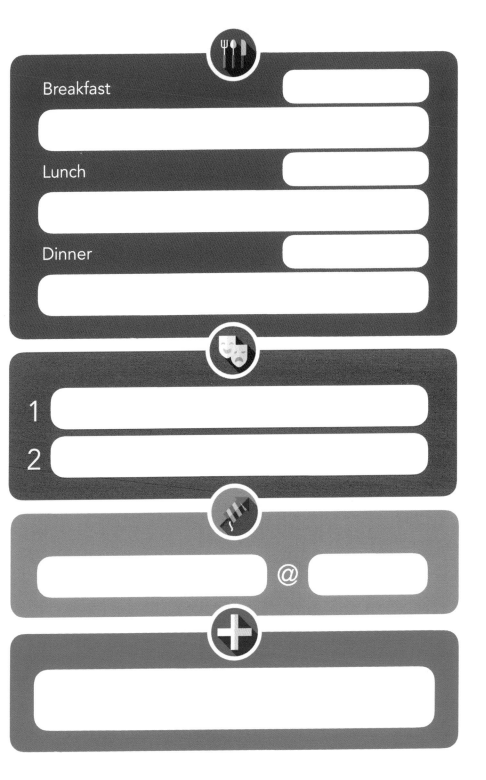

Breakfast

Lunch

Dinner

1

2

@

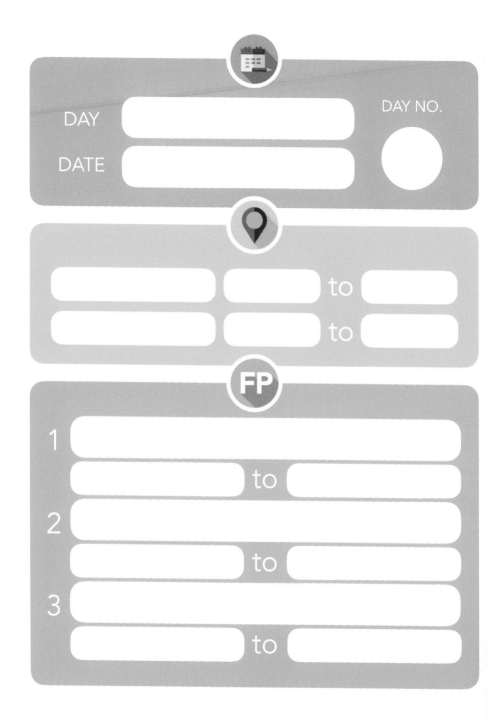

DAY

DATE

DAY NO.

to

to

FP

1

to

2

to

3

to

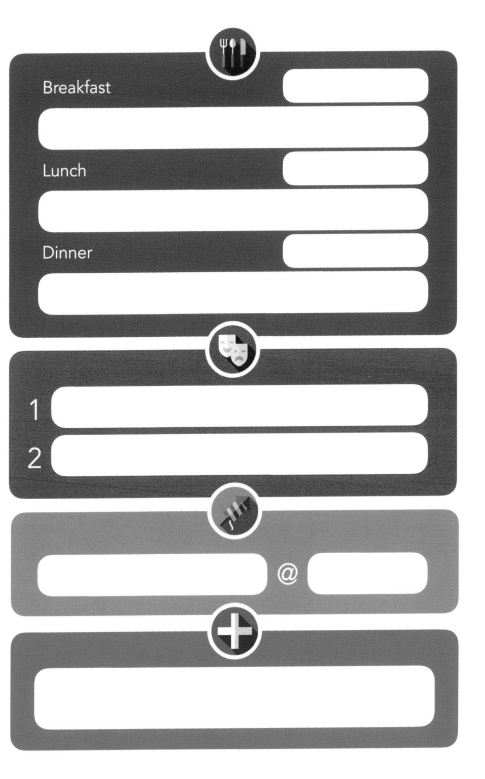

Breakfast

Lunch

Dinner

1
2

@

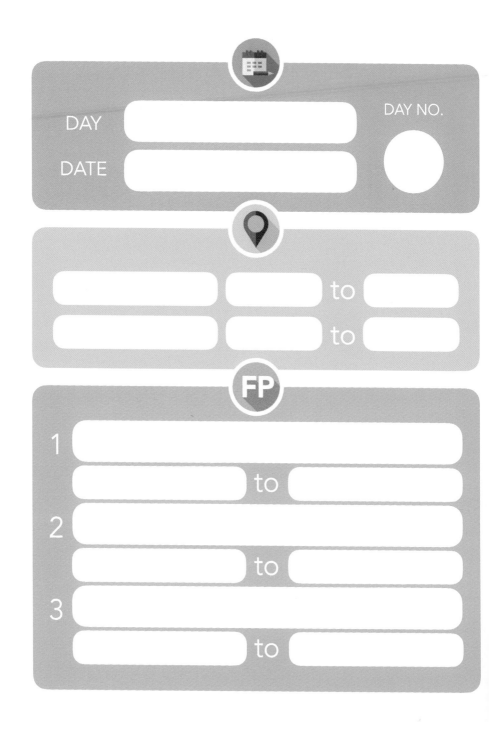

DAY

DATE

DAY NO.

to

to

FP

1

to

2

to

3

to

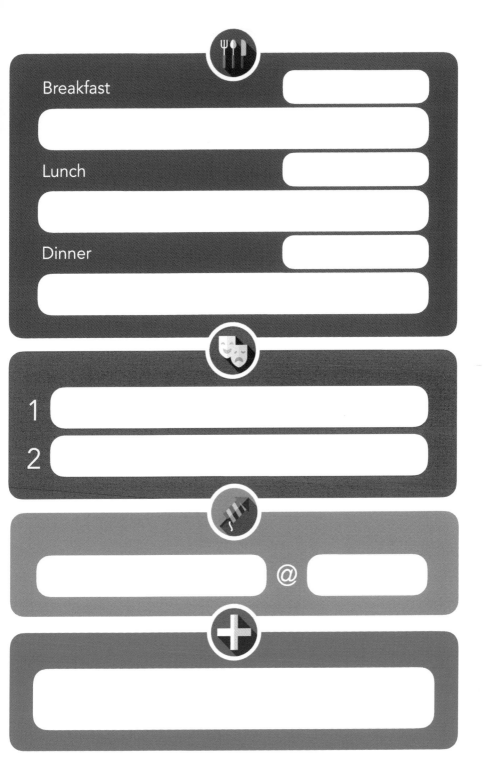

Breakfast

Lunch

Dinner

1
2

@

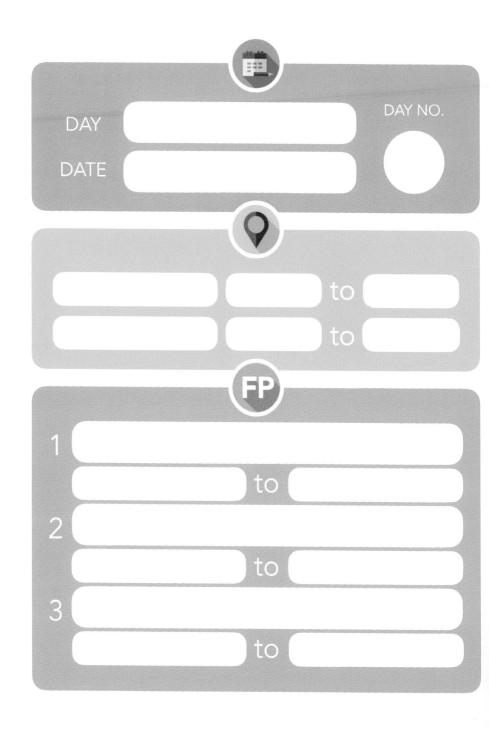

DAY

DATE

DAY NO.

to

to

FP

1

to

2

to

3

to

Breakfast

Lunch

Dinner

1

2

@

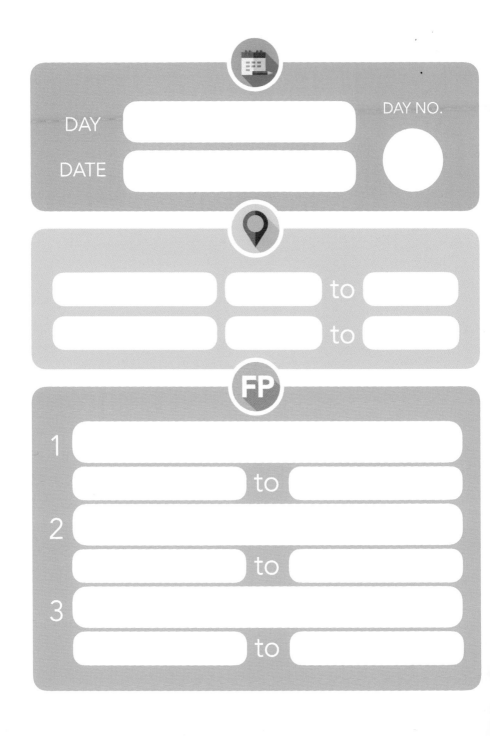

DAY

DATE

DAY NO.

to

to

FP

1

to

2

to

3

to

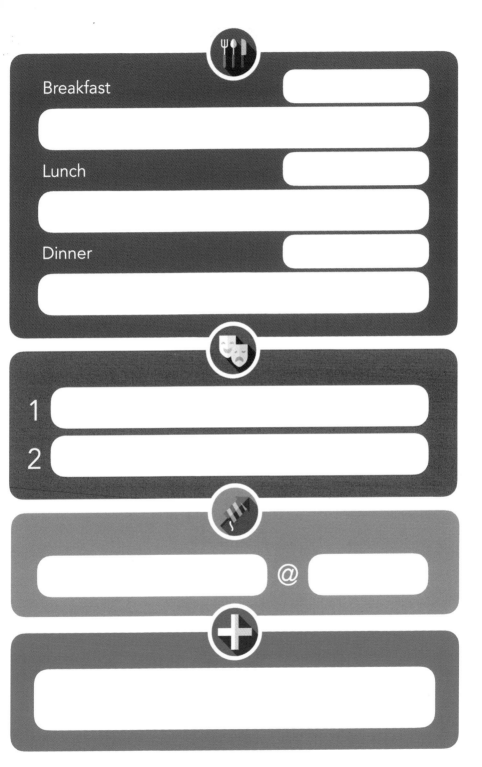

Breakfast

Lunch

Dinner

1

2

@

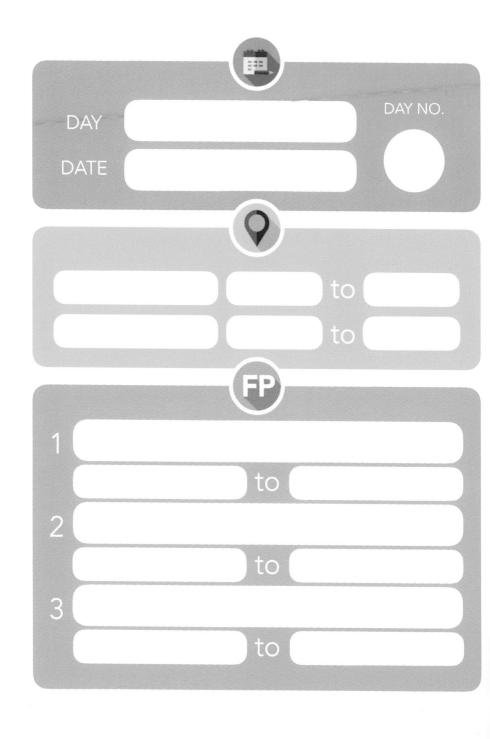

DAY

DATE

DAY NO.

to

to

FP

1

to

2

to

3

to

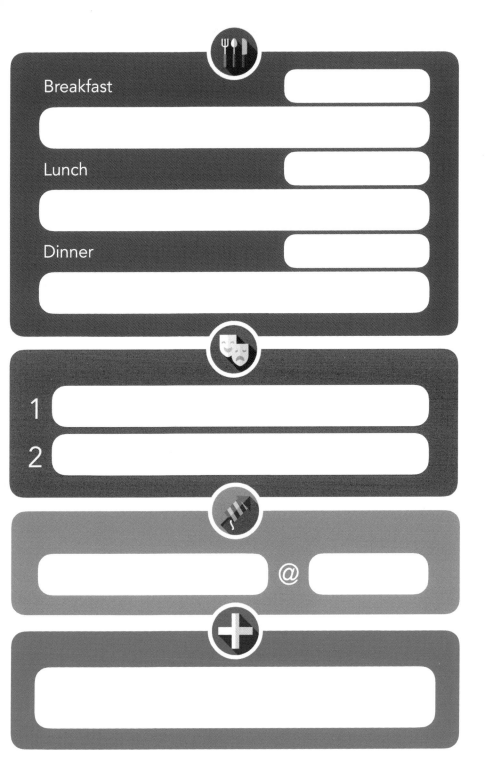

Breakfast

Lunch

Dinner

1

2

@

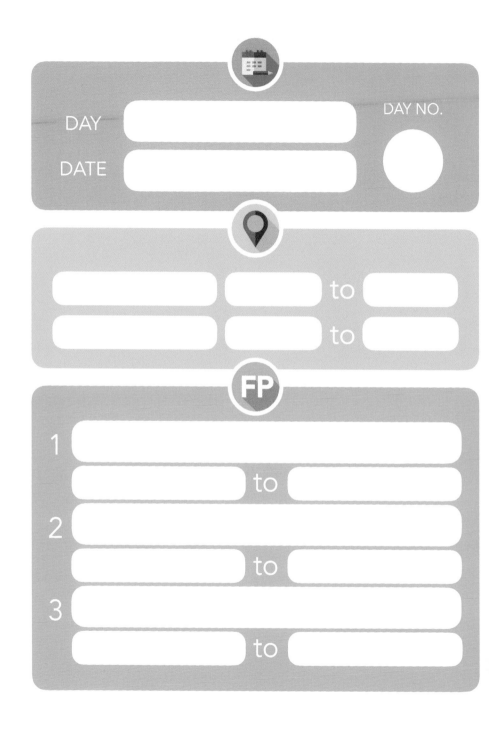

DAY

DATE

DAY NO.

to

to

1

to

2

to

3

to

Breakfast

Lunch

Dinner

1

2

@

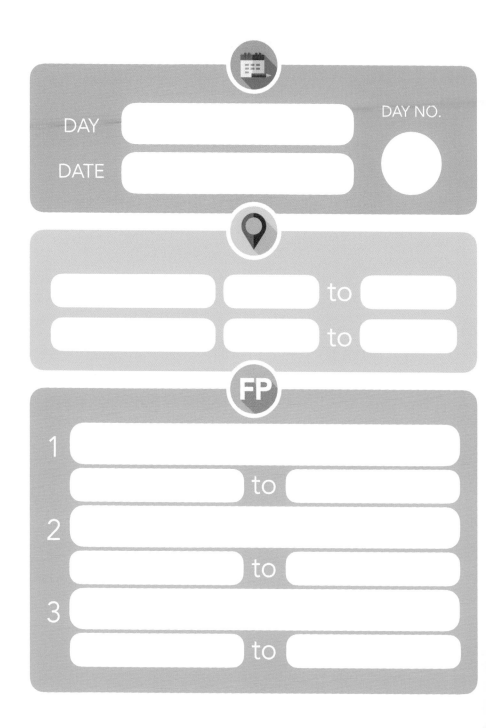

DAY

DATE

DAY NO.

to

to

FP

1

to

2

to

3

to

Breakfast

Lunch

Dinner

1

2

@

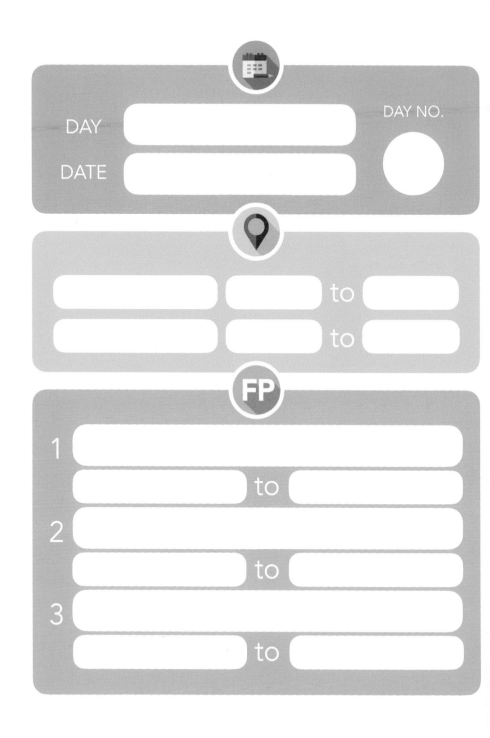

DAY

DATE

DAY NO.

to

to

FP

1

to

2

to

3

to

Breakfast

Lunch

Dinner

1

2

@

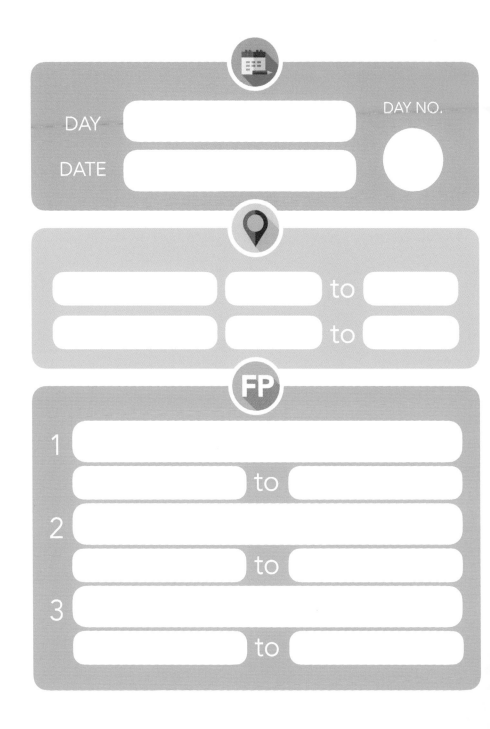

DAY

DATE

DAY NO.

to

to

1

to

2

to

3

to

Breakfast

Lunch

Dinner

1

2

@

Essential Packing

What I need to pack, tends to come to me at various moments in the lead-up to my vacation (normally right before I fall asleep). Here's some space to note down what you're taking.

There's also space for you to check each item off once you've bought it/got it and check it off once it's safely in a bag and ready to go to Disney!

ITEM	GOT	PACKED

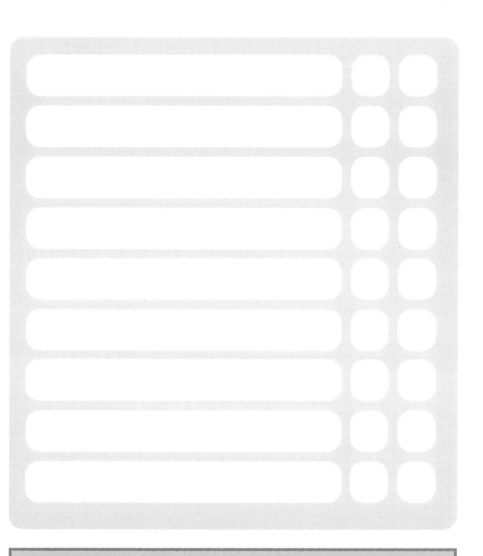

PRO TIP

Fancy having some essentials in your room, like snacks and bottles of water? Consider making an Amazon order to your resort hotel. It'll be held at the front desk for you and will only cost a $6 handling fee.

Call the resort ahead of time to find out their delivery address (different from Google) and make sure you don't schedule delivery for more than a week before your arrival.

FUN FACT

Up for a challenge? Make your way to the Tangled toilets area in Magic Kingdom. In that area you'll find 10 hidden Pascal chameleons. They're not easy to find but I'll give you the one I found hardest to find… Up in the purple flower bed above the entrance to the ladies'.

PRO TIP

On mornings where one of the parks is open for Extra Magic Hours, consider visiting one of the other parks for opening. All the early risers will be attracted to the park with Extra Magic Hours, meaning that the other parks will be considerably quieter at the time of opening.

Countdown

Now the majority of your trip is planned, you can relax and start getting excited for your dream vacation! Below is your 100 days until Disney countdown. Simply cross off the days as you get closer and closer to the magic!

100	99	98	97	96	95	94	93	92	91
90	89	88	87	86	85	84	83	82	81
80	79	78	77	76	75	74	73	72	71
70	69	68	67	66	65	64	63	62	61
60	59	58	57	56	55	54	53	52	51
50	49	48	47	46	45	44	43	42	41
40	39	38	37	36	35	34	33	32	31
30	29	28	27	26	25	24	23	22	21
20	19	18	17	16	15	14	13	12	11
10	9	8	7	6	5	4	3	2	1

Let's go to Walt Disney World

Here's a space for anything else…

Have a Magical Time

Hopefully, you're all set for your dream Walt Disney World vacation!

Thank you for choosing Dream Planner to assist with your vacation planning! It's with this that I shall wish you and your family the most magical time.

Walt Disney World is a place where you get the chance to be a kid again, forget about the worries of the world and immerse yourself in the magic of Disney. Count down the days until you get there and don't let a moment pass you by once you're in the magic.

Have a magical vacation and thank you for your support!

- Adam

DREAM PLANNER

A Planner for Your Dream Walt Disney
World Vacation

It's time to plan your dream Walt Disney World vacation!
With so much to see and do, it's essential to have a plan
of which park you're going to, where you'd like to dine
and which attractions are your priority.

Dream Planner is the must have planner for any family going to
Walt Disney World. Whether it's your 1st or 51st time, you'll be
able to enjoy the planning process as a family, deciding on what
you'd love to do and what you'll actually have time for.

Adam Hattan's Dream Planner is best used alongside
his tips and advice book, *Dream Guide: An Unofficial
Guide to Walt Disney World in Florida*. Available to
purchase from www.adamhattan.com.

UK £7.99

ISBN 978-1-9160897-0-9

9 781916 089709 >

The *Hattan* Company

www.thehattancompany.com   © The Hattan Company 2019   Printed in the UK

Watch Adam's Vlogs at YouTube.com/adamhattan

DREAM PLANNER

A Planner for Your Dream Walt Disney World Vacation

by Adam Hattan

This **DREAM PLANNER** belongs to...

INTRODUCTION

You're going to Walt Disney World!

Whether you've only just decided when you're going or you're now counting down the days until your magical vacation begins, this planner is here to help you get all kinds of excited for your trip!

Not only that, the tools within this planner will help you plan your dream vacation down to the very last fast pass.

If you're like me, you've probably spent a few hours lying awake at night, just dreaming about all the magical experiences that await you in Walt Disney World. Maybe it's your favourite attraction, the taste of your favourite Disney snack or perhaps it's your resort hotel room that you just can't wait to relax in?

Well the fun starts now! Planning the magic you're going to have is a big part of what makes a Walt Disney World vacation so exciting. Planning isn't only exciting, it's also highly necessary. With so many attractions, dining options, shows and more to choose from... you've got some decisions to make before you arrive in Orlando.

If you've already bought my *Dream Guide: An Unofficial Guide to Walt Disney World in Florida*, you're already at an advantage. I'll be directing you to certain pages within *Dream Guide* later on. This is to hopefully make your planning process as easy as possible, without leaving you in the dark on particular topics. If you haven't bought your *Dream Guide* yet, you can do so at www.adamhattan.com.

Where do you want to go? What do you want to do? How would you like to enjoy your vacation? It's all up to you now, as you put your Dream Planner to work in making your dream vacation a reality.

Happy planning!

- Adam

Hattan Publishing
PO Box 759
Banbury
OX16 6PQ
United Kingdom

ISBN: 978-1-9160897-0-9

For information about custom editions, special sales, premium or corporate purchases, please contact The Hattan Company at *contact@adamhattan.com*